Anette Ruberg-Neuser

School on Fire:
A Crime Story

W0174568

verlag

Impressum

School on Fire: A Crime Story

Anette Ruberg-Neuser (Jahrgang 1961) ist Konrektorin an einer Grund- und Verbundenen Haupt- und Realschule in Hessen. In den vergangenen Jahren hat sie umfangreiches Unterrichtsmaterial für Haupt- und Realschulklassen der Jahrgangsstufen 5–10 erstellt und veröffentlicht.

2. Auflage 2016
© 2016 AOL-Verlag, Hamburg
AAP Lehrerfachverlage GmbH
Alle Rechte vorbehalten.

Veritaskai 3 · 21079 Hamburg
Fon (040) 32 50 83-060 · Fax (040) 32 50 83-050 · info@aol-verlag.de · www.aol-verlag.de

Redaktion: Kathrin Roth
Layout/Satz: Satzpunkt Ursula Ewert GmbH, Bayreuth
Coverfoto: arturas kerdokas – Fotolia.com

ISBN: 978-3-403-10372-1

Engagiert unterrichten. Natürlich lernen.

Inhaltsverzeichnis

1. Outside

"Bye mum. I'm going for my walk", Phil shouted from the hall to the kitchen where her mother was preparing dinner.

"Okay, darling. Dinner is in about 45 minutes.
5 Don't be late", Mrs Doherty, Phil's mother, answered.

"No, mum, I'll be on time."

Phil opened the door and walked into the cool evening. It was a Friday in late October, and the
10 days were getting shorter, so at 6:30 pm it was already beginning to get dark.

Phil's full Christian name was Philippa Elizabeth, after her two grandmothers. But
15 everybody called her Phil. She did not like her nickname because it was actually a boy's short name for Philip, but Phil was a
20 lot better than her full Christian names, which she absolutely hated.

Phil was overweight, and she had been suffering from
25 diabetes for a few years.

5

Every day she had to inject insulin, which helped her stay strong and gave her energy. In the past, being overweight was never really a problem for Phil. She loved her food after a long and tiring day at school. Her favourites were chocolate and potato crisps, which she ate while watching films on TV after school or at the weekends.

But when she turned 15 and found that all her classmates were dating their first boyfriends, she decided to lose weight because slim girls had better chances to get boyfriends. She fancied Dean, a boy in her class. Dean did not have a girlfriend, but Phil knew he also liked slim girls.

Over the last two months Phil had lost 16 pounds. She had stopped eating crisps, and she only ate one small piece of chocolate every day. She discovered that apples, bananas and oranges tasted good, and in the school cafeteria she preferred a fresh salad to chips with ketchup and mayonnaise.

In the evenings after her homework she liked doing power walking in the park near her neighbourhood. Walking helped Phil lose weight more quickly, and it helped her work off school stress or the annoying arguments she always had with Natalie, her thirteen year old and much slimmer sister.

On her way to the park, Phil passed Park High School, a comprehensive school where all the

boys and girls of this part of the town went. Phil
55 liked her school. It had been renovated two years
ago. Inside the halls and classrooms were brightly
coloured. As a member of the Redecorating Club
she had helped to decorate some of the halls and
classrooms. She had painted bright yellow suns
60 and blue and red flowers on the walls. It had been
great fun.

Phil looked into the sky. Big, heavy clouds hung
over her school and the park ahead, and she
feared that it would start to rain any minute.

65 Suddenly there was a flash of lightning and not
long after that the sound of rolling thunder.

"Oh, damn!" Phil shouted to herself. "Why didn't I
put on my mackintosh? If it starts raining now I'll
be wet and soaked within minutes." Then the first
70 big raindrops began to fall.

Phil stopped walking and looked over to her
school. "I could find shelter under the main
entrance", she thought aloud. She opened the big
school gate and ran towards the entrance. When
75 she reached it her sweat suit was already wet.
Then a heavy storm with lightning, thunder, and
nasty gusts of wind started, and Phil began to feel
very cold.

2. Inside

Phil decided to ring her mother with her mobile phone. Her mother could pick her up in her car and drive her home where she could have a nice hot bath. She pulled her mobile out of her pocket
5 and switched it on. The display flashed for a few seconds, then it went black.

"Damn", Phil shouted. "I forgot to recharge it." Angrily she turned towards the entrance door and banged her fist on it. The door moved and she
10 realized that it was not locked. Phil looked at her watch. It was nearly 7:00 pm. At this time of the day the building was deserted. And Mr Ashton, the caretaker, never forgot to lock the school building. Perhaps he was still inside? She opened

15 the door and went inside, where she soon felt warm and safe. Phil hoped that her mother wasn't too worried. She would have liked to tell her she was okay, but she was sure all rooms with a telephone would be locked.

20 Yet she felt strange inside the building. Everything was quiet. During the day, it was full of noisy pupils running along hallways and shouting in classrooms.

"Hello", she shouted. Perhaps she could find Mr
25 Ashton and use his mobile to call her mum. But there was no answer. "Hello? Mr Ashton?" she shouted again, this time louder. Again nobody answered.

It was getting really dark outside and inside the
30 building, too. The storm was still very heavy. Phil looked for a light switch. She had never switched on a light in the big hallway of Park High School, so she didn't know where to find the switch. She looked around again, but there were no switches
35 anywhere. Perhaps Mr Ashton switched on the lights from his office.

She sat down on one of the chairs outside the school office. Normally, parents waiting to speak with Mr Cutter, the headmaster, sat there.

40 Flashes of lightning brightened the hallway every few seconds. Thunder rolled loudly and reminded

Phil of a wild animal, looking for her and waiting for her to come out of the school building.

Phil was frightened and started to shiver. She
45 should really call her mum and tell her where she was. She took out her mobile again and shook it fiercely, hoping it would come back to life for just one call. But the display stayed black. "Damn! It's completely dead. You stupid cow", Phil shouted at
50 herself.

She knew that her mum would be dead worried. Even Natalie would be worried. Suddenly Phil heard a noise.

Somewhere in the school someone was shouting.
55 It seemed to come from upstairs, perhaps the first or second floor and it sounded like a man's voice. So Mr Ashton *was* still in the building. And he was upstairs. But why did he shout? Phil got up from her chair and listened.

60 Again somebody shouted, but this time it sounded like a female voice.

"Hello?" Phil shouted. "Who's there?" Nobody answered.

"Hello?" Phil shouted again. "Mr Ashton? Is that
65 you?" Still no answer.

Then Phil noticed something else. She smelled smoke. And the smell was coming from upstairs.

3. Voices

Something was on fire. Phil could smell that. Perhaps a flash of lightning had struck a part of the building. Phil didn't know what to do. Should she try to find out what had happened upstairs?

5 Should she just run out of the building? She was not as scared of thunderstorms as her little sister Natalie, but she didn't want to risk getting struck by lightning. So she decided to find out what had happened upstairs. Perhaps someone was hurt or

10 in danger, and she was the only one who could help. She had not heard any voices for minutes, but she was sure someone was upstairs. Phil was not a very brave girl, and she walked towards the staircase slowly. Only when there was a flash of

15 lightning could she see where she was going.

She found the handrail of the staircase and started to go upstairs. When she reached the first floor she heard something again. Phil stopped to listen. Yes, she could hear voices again and people were

20 running along a corridor.

"Hello, who's there?" she shouted. "Do you need help?" There was no answer. The voices and the running had stopped, too. The smell of smoke was stronger here. Phil felt a cold shiver running down

25 her back. Again she wasn't sure what to do.

There was still a chance to go downstairs and out of the building. She could see that the storm was getting weaker. There wasn't so much thunder and lightning now. But she also felt that something
30 was very wrong on the second floor, and she wanted to find out what it was. So she climbed up the stairs to the second floor. She tried not to make any noises now. Slowly she reached the second floor, where there was more smoke. It was
35 coming from the west wing. Her classroom was in the west wing. She had to find out what had happened.

Slowly she walked in the direction of her classroom. The smoke was getting thicker now
40 and she started to cough.

Then Phil saw a light at the end of the corridor. It wasn't an ordinary light coming from electric light bulbs. There were flames in one of the classrooms. Her classroom. She began to run. Breathing was
45 getting more difficult.

Then she stumbled over something lying in the corridor. She fell and hurt her right shoulder. "Ouch", she shouted. "What was that?" Breathing was very difficult now. She took off her sweat
50 jacket – the movements hurt because of her bruised shoulder – and pressed it to her face. Then she looked at the thing that had caused her to stumble. She screamed. It was a person. It was Mr

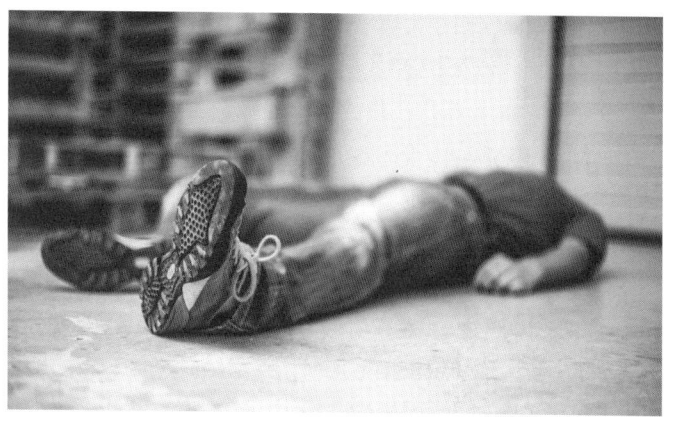

Ashton, and he was unconscious. So it *was* him
who had shouted. Perhaps he had had a heart
attack? Phil didn't know what to do.

"Mr Ashton", Phil shouted. "Mr Ashton, wake up.
We must get out of here!" But Mr Ashton did not
move. He was a heavy man, and Phil couldn't lift
him.

Phil was desperate. Only a few feet away her
classroom was on fire. The smoke made her
cough. She couldn't breathe. She had to get out of
here, but she couldn't leave Mr Ashton in the
corridor.

"Help!" she shouted. "Is anybody there? I need
help! Please!"

Then she noticed a figure watching her from the
other side of the corridor.

4. Worries

Mrs Doherty looked out her kitchen window. She was worried. Where was Phil? When the thunderstorm started she went to the front door. She was sure Phil would come running home

5 quickly because she could not have gone far.

When Phil didn't come after ten minutes, Mrs Doherty tried to call her on her mobile phone. But there was only the voicemail. Had Phil forgotten to switch on her mobile? Mrs Doherty began to think

10 that Phil could have found shelter somewhere. She remembered that there was a sheltered bus stop on the way to the park. Perhaps Phil was sitting in it waiting for the rain to stop. After another

quarter of an hour Mrs Doherty began to ring Phil's
15 friends, Brenda and Sophie, who lived close to the
park, but Phil had not arrived there.

Slowly the thunderstorm got weaker.

The rain stopped pouring down, and Mrs Doherty
stood again at the kitchen window, hoping to see
20 Phil any moment. But she didn't come.

"Where's Phil?" Natalie asked her mother when
she came into the kitchen to drink some milk.
Natalie was afraid of thunderstorms, and she had
spent most of the time in her bed.

25 "I don't know, Natty. But I'm very worried", Mrs
Doherty answered.

"Have you tried her mobile yet?" Natalie suggested.

"Yes, of course. But there was only her voicemail.
Could you try to ring her again, please?"

30 Natalie went to her room and dialled Phil's number.
Phil's mobile rang – but again there was only the
voicemail.

"Mum, it's the voicemail again", Natalie told her
mother. "I think Phil's mobile is off."

35 "Oh no, she must have forgotten to switch it on",
Mrs Doherty said angrily.

"Or her mobile can't get a signal", Natalie said.

"Oh, Natalie, what should we do?" her mother
asked.

40 "We could look for her by car", Natalie suggested.

"Good idea. Bring me the car keys", Mrs Doherty said, "and we will go and look for her now."

Mrs Doherty drove the car out of the garage, and Natalie jumped in. First they drove to the sheltered
45 bus stop where Mrs Doherty had hoped to find Phil. But she wasn't there.

"Where can she be?" Mrs Doherty asked Natalie.

"I've no idea, mum. Perhaps she found shelter under one of the big trees in the park", Natalie
50 replied.

"No, Natty, I don't think she's there. Phil knows that you should never find shelter under a tree in a thunderstorm. It's too dangerous."

They drove past the school. The rain was getting
55 weaker, and it was completely dark.

"Could she be in the school building?" Mrs Doherty asked Natalie.

"I don't think so, mum. They usually lock the building at about 6:00 pm. You can't get in after
60 that", Natalie answered, and she noticed that her mother looked really frightened now.

"Okay", Mrs Doherty said. "Let's drive to the park and look for her there." She parked the car near the entrance to the park. Together they entered
65 the park and walked along the main path. They shouted for Phil, but there was no answer.

Suddenly Mrs Doherty sat down on one of the wet benches and began to cry. She was desperate. "Where's my baby?" she sobbed.

70 "Mum", Natalie said. "Please don't cry. We'll find her. Perhaps she has arrived home while we have been out here looking for her. Come on, mum. You'll catch a cold sitting on that wet bench.

"Alright, let's go home. But if she hasn't arrived
75 home yet, I'll call the hospital. And we shouldn't hesitate too long to call the police", Mrs Doherty said.

5. Blow

The smoke was burning in her eyes and she had to cough.

"Who's there?" Phil shouted. The figure didn't move.

5 "Come and help me. Mr Ashton is unconscious", Phil cried. Still the figure didn't move. What's going on here?, Phil thought. I don't understand a thing. She was surprised when she could suddenly make out two more figures. They stared at Phil, who was
10 still kneeling next to Mr Ashton, and Phil stared at them. Then the first figure slowly moved towards her.

"Don't!" one of the other figures shouted. It was a girl. Her voice sounded familiar to Phil, but she
15 couldn't remember whose voice it was. The first figure was still moving towards her.

The way the figure walked looked familiar to her, too.

The fire had reached the wall outside her classroom.
20 The flames were licking the new wallpaper. Soon they would reach one of the bright yellow suns Phil had painted.

There was enough light in the hall now that Phil could get a glimpse of the figure's face. It was a
25 young man's face. A familiar face. A face she liked.

"Dean?" she said. "Is that you?"

"Don't talk! We must get out of here!" the girl shouted. Then she coughed.

"Dean?" Phil asked again, but the figure didn't say
30 anything. Was it really possible that the boy she liked most in her class had set their classroom on fire?

"Leave them alone", the girl warned. "And let's get out of here quickly. The whole corridor will be on
35 fire soon."

"We can't leave them here", the boy croaked. Was it Dean's voice? Phil was not sure.

"Perhaps *you* can't, but *we* can, can't we?" the girl said and turned to the third figure. Then she quickly
40 walked towards Phil.

Who is that girl?, Phil thought. I'm sure I know her voice, but I can't put a name to her.

Suddenly Phil felt a terrible blow on her head. Then everything went dark.

6. Emergencies

After Mr Doherty had come home from work and
learned about Phil's disappearance the Dohertys
decided to call the police.

Police Sergeant Cooper and Police Constable
5 Miller arrived at the Dohertys' house.

The two police officers sat at the kitchen table.
They asked the Dohertys what Phil looked like and
what she was wearing that evening.

"Well, she's about 5'6", not too slim, perhaps
10 12 stone. She's got shoulder-length strawberry
blond her, and she is wearing her white and pink
sweat suit. Nothing special", Mrs Doherty said
and started to cry again.

"Don't be so upset, Linda", Mr Doherty said and
15 took her in his arms. "I'm sure there is a simple
explanation why she hasn't come home yet."

"Have you called the hospital yet?" Police Sergeant
Cooper asked. "Perhaps she had an accident."

"Of course. That was the first thing I did after we
20 came home from our first search. But they didn't
have anybody with an accident tonight. Oh God,
perhaps she *did* have an accident in the park and
is now lying somewhere helpless and wet." More
tears rolled down Mrs Doherty's cheeks.

"Hasn't your daughter got a mobile?" Constable Miller asked. "Young people usually don't leave the house without their mobiles."

"I've checked that", Natalie answered. "I tried to call her, but I only got her voicemail. But she must have taken it with her. It's not in her room."

"Alright", Police Sergeant Cooper said. "Perhaps there is no signal. We'll ask for more officers from the police station and build a search party. You can join us, of course, and together we'll look for Philippa in the park and in the area around her school."

"Of course we'll be a part of the search party", Mr Doherty said.

"Okay, then you'd better take a torch with you", the sergeant said. He went to his car and radioed the police station to get help for the search party.

A short time later the Dohertys and two policecars arrived at the entrance to the park. It was a search party of seven: the family and four policemen.

They had just switched on their torches to look for Phil in the park when a fire siren began to wail.

"There must be a fire", Police Sergeant Cooper said and went back to his car to radio back to the police station for information.

"They said someone called because Park High School was on fire", he said when he came back to his waiting colleagues and the Dohertys.

"We have to check on that first, I'm afraid", he said.

55 The school was about 200 yards on the right. At first the Dohertys and the police officers couldn't see any sign of a fire. But suddenly they heard a whoomph and flames were shooting out of the roof and out of some windows on the second floor.

60 "My God", Natalie said. "My school is burning. That's unbelievable."

Now two fire engines arrived and drove onto the school yard.

"Okay", said the sergeant who had radioed his
65 station. "Constable Miller and Constable Turner, you'll go with the Dohertys and look for Philippa. Constable Weaver, we'll have a look at the fire."

7. Looking for answers

After two hours the fire at Park High School was under control. The fire had started in one of the classrooms on the second floor and spread to the corridor, and from there to two more classrooms.
5 The fire brigade also found the caretaker unconscious in a science room, which had not yet caught fire. He had a big head wound and a severe smoke poisoning. He was taken to hospital and his condition was life-threatening.
10 Police and fire brigade found out that the fire was caused by several old petrol-soaked T-shirts that were set on fire. They had been put under the teacher's desk, under shelves, inside a cupboard and into a bin.

15 The arsonists must have entered through the main entrance, which had not yet been locked by the caretaker. While they were setting the classroom on fire on the second floor Mr Ashton must have discovered them, and they knocked him

20 unconscious. There were no clues of who started the fire, but the police believed that it must have been pupils.

The search party in the park was not successful. They couldn't find Phil anywhere. The Dohertys

25 were very upset. They had hoped to find Phil there, hurt perhaps, but now they didn't know where their daughter could be. They had no idea where else to look for her. They had phoned all her friends. Mrs Doherty rang the hospital for a second

30 time, but Phil had not been taken in.

Later that evening Mr and Mrs Doherty drove to the police station to file a missing person's report. They spoke to Detective Inspector Garner.

"Does Phil have any problems at school?"

35 Detective Inspector Garner asked.

"No, of course not", Mrs Doherty answered. "She has never had any problems. She is a good student and she has many friends."

"Are there any problems at home, Mrs Doherty?"

40 the Detective Inspector wanted to know.

"No, everything is fine", Mrs Doherty said. "Phil is a very uncomplicated person. We have always talked about everything. And she has a good relationship to Natalie, her younger sister."

45 "So you can't think of any reason why she could have run away?" the Detective Inspector went on.

"No, of course not", Mrs Doherty answered angrily. "I saw her purse in her room. So she left the house without any money. A girl who wants to run away

50 doesn't leave without her purse."

"Yes, you're right", the Detective Inspector said. "We might have to consider kidnapping."

"Kidnapping?" Mr and Mrs Doherty shouted at the same time.

55 "Well", Detective Inspector Garner began, "if she hasn't come home by now, and if we haven't found her here in town, and if she hasn't run away, there is hardly any other possibility."

Mrs Doherty began to cry. "Oh no. Where's my

60 baby?"

"There must be something that you can do", Mr Doherty said. He was also very worried now.

Detective Inspector Garner looked at them for a long time. Then he said: "Well, we can wait until
65 somebody calls you and asks for a ransom. I'll send over one of our constables who will stay at your house overnight. And we will send Phil's photo to all police stations nationwide, to train stations and airports. In addition we let the local
70 radio and TV stations put it in their news."

"Is there anything *we* can do?" Mr Doherty asked. "Sure, you could think of more people where Phil could have found shelter during the thunderstorm and of people to whom she could have gone –
75 grandparents, uncles, aunts, friends and so on. And you could design a missing person poster which you can distribute in shops and in the neighbourhood."

Suddenly Mrs Doherty put a hand over her mouth
80 and shrieked. "Oh my god!"

"What?" Mr Doherty and Detective Inspector Garner both asked at the same time.

"We've completely forgotten about Phil's diabetes. She needs injections!"

85 "When is the next injection due?" Detective Inspector Garner asked.

"Normally she needs her injection in the morning before she goes to school", Mr Doherty answered.

"So we've still got some hours before her next injection is due", the Detective Inspector said.

"What will happen, if she doesn't get her insulin?"

"She won't feel well. She'll feel weak, extremely tired and she could even fall into a coma", Mrs Doherty said and began to sob. Mr Doherty took her in his arms.

"We'll find her. I promise", he said, trying to console his wife.

8. Darkness

Phil had a terrible headache. Carefully she opened her eyes and – darkness. She lifted her head. Was she blind? What had happened to her? She tried to remember, but her head was hurting so much.

5 So she put it down again on the cold hard floor for another five minutes. Then slowly everything came back to her.

summary

There was a thunderstorm. She wanted to find shelter under the main entrance. She found the

10 door open. There were no lights. She heard voices and thought it was Mr Ashton, the caretaker. Then she smelled smoke and walked up the stairs to the second floor. She remembered that her classroom was on fire. And there was somebody lying in

15 the corridor – it was Mr Ashton. He was unconscious. Then there were those three figures. She was sure she knew

20 one of them – Dean. And she was sure she knew the girl's voice, too. She remembered that she talked to them, and

25 then suddenly she didn't

remember anything. Someone had given her a hard blow on the head. Was it Dean, the girl or the third person she could not see clearly? Phil couldn't remember. What had happened to Mr

30 Ashton? And what about the fire? And most important of all, where was she now?

"Hello?" she croaked. Her voice wasn't strong enough. There was no answer.

"Hello?" she tried to shout, but her voice was too

35 weak.

She could still smell smoke, but the smell wasn't strong, so she must be far away from the fire.

She tried to figure out where she was. She lay on a cold and hard floor of a completely dark room.

40 There weren't any windows, so it wasn't a classroom.

Phil sat up, then she turned on her hands and knees. Carefully she crawled around the room. She touched the legs of tables and chairs. She

45 had to be in a storeroom. Phil knew that the storerooms of Park High School were in the basement. I must find the door, Phil thought. Then I can bang on it, and perhaps somebody will hear me. Slowly she explored the room. Twice she hurt

50 her head when she ran into objects which she could not identify. Then she touched a wall. I must move along the wall if I want to find the door, she

thought. But more objects blocked her way, and she had to move around them.

55 Finally she reached the door. It was a metal door. She stood up. When she was standing on her legs she felt very weak. Her head hurt even more and she felt dizzy. She found the handle and pushed it down – locked. Someone had locked her inside

60 this storeroom. Perhaps there is a light switch, she then thought. With her hands she searched for it on the walls next to the door. But she couldn't touch any. The switch must be on the outside she realized.

65 She banged with both her fists at the door and shouted for help. From time to time she stopped banging and shouting and listened. But she only heard silence. Nobody heard her. Nobody would open the door. Nobody knew she was down here.

70 With her back against the door Phil sat down on the cold floor. She wished she could lie in her warm and comfortable bed. She wished she could be in her mum's arms. She wished she had recharged the batteries of her mobile.

75 Where was it anyway? It was no longer in her pocket. She must have lost it.

Then she began to sob.

9. Guilt

"Why did you save that fat cow and that idiot Ashton?" Cindy was angry. "You could have left them in the corridor."

Dean, Cindy and Matt had watched the fire brigade
5 fighting the fire from a safe distance. Now they were sitting at a corner table in a snack bar eating burgers.

"Are you nuts, Cindy?" Dean answered. "They could have died."

10 "Correct", Matt said. "But you saved them. And now they can tell the police that *we* started the fire."

"We can't know that", Dean said.

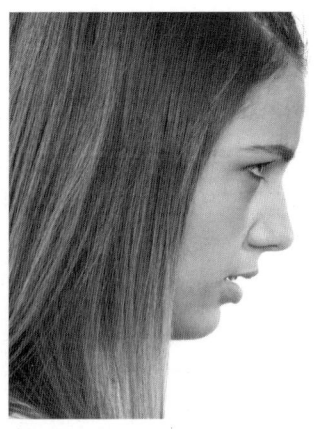
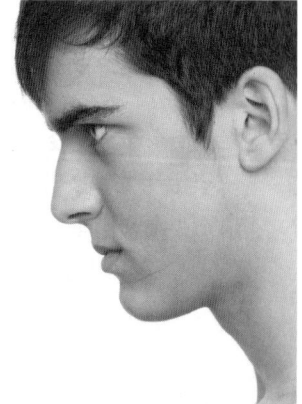

"Of course we can", Cindy replied. "Even if Ashton
15 didn't recognize us, that fat cow certainly did. At
least she recognized you, Dean."

"She couldn't see me clearly, so she probably only
thought she had seen me", Dean answered.

"Don't be stupid", Cindy said. "You talked to me in
20 the corridor. I'm sure she recognized you."

"Okay, maybe she saw me, but I can always say it
wasn't me. And by the way, you talked to me, too.
Have you forgotten? Maybe she recognized your
voice, too", Dean said.

25 "No", Cindy answered. "We don't care about each
other and we never talk, not even in class. I'm sure
she doesn't even know what I look like."

"The police will ask for an alibi", Matt said. "What
will you tell them?"

30 "That's no problem", Dean said. "We can tell them
we were all watching DVDs at my house. My
parents aren't at home over the weekend, so
nobody can say we weren't there."

"I hope you're right", Cindy said. "I still think you
35 should have left Ashton and that girl in the corridor.
Then we wouldn't have to think about alibis."

"Oh, shut up", Dean replied. "I already regret that I
agreed to your idea to set fire to the school. It was
a stupid plan."

40 "Oh, really?" Matt said. "Who said it would be best
to burn the place to ashes? And who couldn't wait

to see the stupid faces of that idiot Cutter and the rest of those teacher swines?"

"Alright, alright, *I* did", Dean answered. "But I
45 changed my mind. I never wanted to threaten the lives of people. And I don't understand how you can be so cold-hearted. I wish I had never done what I did tonight."

With that said Dean stood up and walked out of
50 the snack bar.

10. Dreams

Phil was in the corridor again. Flames were coming out of her classroom and crawling along the walls of the corridor. Her wonderful paintings on the special wallpaper were quickly burning away and
5 left nasty black marks on the wall.

The air was full of thick smoke and she could hardly breathe. Every few seconds she coughed.

Phil tried to lift Mr Ashton. She couldn't leave him in the corridor. But he was too heavy.

10 "Help me, please", she shouted, but none of the three figures watching her from the other end of the corridor moved.

"Why don't you help me?" she shouted again. "He will die if you don't!" Again nobody moved.

15 Phil grabbed Mr Ashton's ankles and slowly dragged him along the corridor, away from the flames and the smoke. She had to stop when the coughing fits came. But she didn't give up. Then she passed the three dark figures. They wore
20 sweatshirts with big hoods, which they had pulled deep into their faces. They didn't move. They just stood there like statues. Phil tried to look into their faces. Cold eyes stared back at her, but she didn't recognize any of their faces.

²⁵ When she had passed them with Mr Ashton they slowly began to follow her.

"Help me!" she pleaded again. "Can't you see that Mr Ashton is in danger? We're all in danger!"

The figures only stared at her and slowly followed.

³⁰ When Phil was close to the top of the stairs the three figures suddenly moved forward. Phil shrieked and let go of Mr Ashton's ankles. Two of the figures grabbed her and pulled her to the top of the stairs. Then the third figure pushed her hard ³⁵ and she fell down the stairs.

Phil woke up with a start. Where was she?

Then she remembered. She was still trapped in that dark room. She was shivering. Cold sweat was on her forehead, and the floor where she was

40 lying was wet. Slowly she realized what had happened. While she was asleep she had wet herself. She felt embarrassed. This had never happened to her before. Her underwear and the pants of her sweat suit were soaked, and she felt
45 very uncomfortable. There was nothing she could do but move to a dry spot in the room.

She felt dizzy and a new headache started. She was hungry and thirsty and felt very tired.

What time was it? Was it already Saturday?

50 She needed her injection. She needed something to eat and drink. She knew that if she didn't get any of this she could fall into a coma.

New tears welled up in her eyes. Why didn't anybody come to find her?

11. Bad conscience

Dean woke up at 4:30 am. It was too early to get up on a Saturday morning, so he lay awake in his bed. He thought about last night, about the fire that he, Cindy and Matt had started at their school.
5 It was all because they had problems with Mr Hardy, their maths teacher, who had written letters to their parents after they had misbehaved in maths lessons and stopped doing their homework. Mr Hardy had warned them they wouldn't pass
10 their GCSEs in a few months. Then Mr Cutter, the headmaster, had threatened to expel them from school if they misbehaved again. Dean's father was so angry with him that he took away Dean's motorcycle.
15 It was Cindy's idea to stay in their classroom after lessons on Friday and wait until Mr Ashton had left. They soaked some old T-shirts with petrol that Matt had stolen from his father's garage. Unfortunately the caretaker wanted to repair a
20 light in their classroom. That's when he discovered the three pupils.
"What the heck are you doing here?" he asked.
"Waiting for Santa Claus", Cindy answered.
"Seriously", said Mr Ashton, "what are you up to?"
25 Then he smelled the petrol.

"What is going on?" he asked. "I can smell petrol."

"We're planning a barbecue and we've invited the whole class. Wanna come too, Ashton? You can bring the beer", Matt said and slowly stood up

30 from his chair. He went to the cupboard in the back of the classroom, opened it and took out his cricket bat. He was a member of the school cricket team and always kept his bat in the cupboard.

"I think it'll be best if you leave the classroom and

35 the school building at once or I will call Mr Cutter and the police", Mr Ashton threatened.

Just then Matt came towards the caretaker with his bat at the ready.

Mr Ashton saw what was coming. He dropped his

40 tool case.

"Wait, you can't do that. Help", he shouted. Then he ran out of the classroom into the corridor.

But Matt was much faster. In the corridor he caught the caretaker and hit him on the head. Mr Ashton

45 fell down unconscious.

"Quick", Matt shouted when he came back into the classroom. Let's do what we have to do, and then let's get out of here."

Dean ran into the corridor to check on the caretaker.

50 "Are you nuts, Matt?" he shouted. "You probably killed him."

"Don't be such a sissy, Dean," Cindy answered. "Matt only knocked him out. He'll come around soon and can run away from the fire."

55 Dean felt sorry for Mr Ashton. He liked him because he was always nice to all pupils. But he went back into the classroom and watched Matt start the fire with his lighter. The furniture in the classroom started to burn, and quickly the room was full of

60 hot, thick smoke. The three friends left their classroom, went to the other end of the corridor and watched the corridor and neighbouring classroom burst into flames.

Then Phil suddenly appeared. First Dean could

65 not understand why she was inside the school building. Later he realized that Phil must have come inside to get out of the thunderstorm.

After Matt had hit her with his bat, too, he and Cindy wanted to get out of the school as quickly

70 as possible. Dean followed them downstairs to the first floor. But then he suddenly returned to Mr Ashton and Phil. He dragged the caretaker to the science room, which was the room furthest from the burning classrooms. Then he shouldered Phil

75 who was really heavy and carried her downstairs into the hall. Here Cindy and Matt were waiting for him.

"What do you think you're doing?" Matt shouted. "You cannot save her. She'll tell the police everything."

"I couldn't leave her upstairs", Dean shouted back. "We cannot kill her."

"Okay", Cindy said. "Lock her up somewhere."

"Carry her downstairs to the storerooms and lock her in one of them", Matt suggested.

"We can't do that", Dean answered. "She needs food and drink."

"Does she?" Cindy said sarcastically. "I think it'll do her good if she doesn't eat for a few days. She'll lose some weight. We are doing her a favour."

"What if the school burns down completely?" Dean asked. "She'll die, if nobody finds her in time."

"Well", Matt answered. "I don't think that the school will suffer so much damage, but I'm afraid we'll have to take that risk now."

The three of them carried Phil down to the basement where they found a dark storeroom without a window.

"By the way", Cindy said. "Have you saved that blockhead Ashton, too?"

"Well", Dean began. "I ... I dragged him into the science room."

"You idiot", Cindy and Matt shouted at the same time.

12. Clues

Mr and Mrs Doherty didn't sleep all night. A police constable had arrived at their house at 10:30 pm. Together they sat in the living room waiting for the telephone to ring. But nobody rang demanding a
5 ransom for Phil. Mr Doherty kept making coffee to keep the police constable, his wife and himself awake.

Natalie had gone to bed after midnight. But she couldn't sleep well. She often woke up and thought
10 of Phil.

At 7:00 in the morning Mr Doherty called Police Inspector Garner, but there was no news.

The police wanted to find the arsonists. By 8:00 am they started to ask the people in the
15 neighbourhood of the school, but nobody had seen anybody or heard anything. Nobody had been out in the thunderstorm. Windows and doors had been locked.

They scanned the school building and hoped to
20 find clues that would lead them to the arsonists. In the classroom where the fire had started they didn't find anything apart from the charcoaled T-shirts that had been soaked with petrol.

But then a police officer found a pink and white
25 mobile in a corner of the corridor not far from the
staircase.

"It could belong to one of the arsonists", Police
Sergeant Cooper said. "We must recharge it, find
out the pin code, and then we'll know more."

30 Three hours later they knew – thanks to an IT
expert at the police station – that the mobile
belonged to Philippa Doherty, the missing girl.

Police Sergeant Cooper drove to the Dohertys'
house and showed it to Mrs and Mr Doherty and
35 they recognized it at once.

"Yes, that's Phil's mobile. She likes pink", Mrs
Doherty said.

"We found it in the school corridor, not far from the
destroyed classrooms", Police Sergeant Cooper
40 said.

"You don't mean to tell us that you suspect Phil. She didn't have anything to do with the fire", Mr Doherty said angrily. "She wouldn't do anything like that. She loves going to that school."

45 "Yes, and she even helped to redecorate the corridors two years ago", Mrs Doherty added. "She wouldn't destroy her pictures."

"Anyway", Police Sergeant Cooper said. "We have to investigate in all directions."

50 Mrs Doherty sat down on a kitchen chair and started to cry. "Phil is no arsonist", she sobbed.

"We'll check her phone calls and her short messages", the sergeant promised. "We'll contact everyone she has contacted within the last few

55 days. Perhaps that will help us to find the truth."

"Wait!" Mr Doherty said. "What about Mr Ashton, the caretaker. Have you asked him about the arsonists? He must have seen them. And I'm sure he didn't see our daughter!"

60 "Well, Mr Doherty", the sergeant began, "there is some sad news." Now Police Sergeant Cooper hesitated. "He died early this morning. His head wound was too serious."

The Dohertys were shocked.

65 "Oh no", Mrs Doherty said. "He was such a nice man. He never deserved that."

"Don't worry, we'll find the people who did that to him", the sergeant answered. "And we'll find out if Philippa was involved or not."

13. Help

Dean couldn't leave Phil in that dark room for a full weekend.

At 1:30 pm he walked to the school building. He was wearing his hooded sweatshirt again, and had drawn the hood deep down into his face.

Police cars were parked in front of the main entrance, and police officers were looking for clues inside. Dean wanted to get inside too, but because of the crime scene tape outside the main entrance and a police constable on guard he couldn't just slip in. Nervously he waited at a distance. There were a few other people watching, too, but nobody took any notice of Dean.

He had a small shopping bag with him filled with some sandwiches, two bottles of lemonade and a torch.

After fifteen minutes of waiting Dean saw that the police constable got a radio message and then went inside the building. That was Dean's chance. Carefully he went to the entrance and looked inside. There were no policemen in the hall. But he could hear voices upstairs on the upper floors. He climbed over the crime scene tape and ran quickly to the stairs down to the basement. Dean decided

25 he had to hide there and wait until the police had left before he could see Phil.

He sat down behind an old locker in the corridor opposite the storeroom where he and the others had locked Phil, and hoped that the policemen
30 wouldn't look for clues in the basement. They could find him easily.

Dean wondered if Phil was asleep because he couldn't hear any noises from inside the storeroom. Perhaps she had shouted for help and given up
35 when nobody came.

At 3:15 pm Dean heard that the police were leaving the building. He could also hear Mr Cutter's voice. The headmaster wanted to look at the damage, of course. And he would lock the entrance door
40 because Mr Ashton was in hospital.

Dean waited for another ten minutes. He made sure his hood covered most of his face before he unlocked the door to the storeroom. He switched on his torch and lit inside. There was a bad smell
45 in the room, and at first he couldn't find Phil.

Then he saw her. She was lying on the floor in the middle of the room. She didn't move. Was she asleep?

Dean was suddenly worried. Carefully he knelt
50 down next to her and touched her forehead. He could feel cold sweat.

"Phil", he whispered. Phil didn't move.

"Phil", he whispered again, this time louder.

Phil's eyes slowly opened and she tried to move
her head towards Dean, but she was too weak.

"Who's there?" she asked.

Dean didn't answer. He didn't want Phil to
recognize him.

"Help me, please", Phil said weakly. "I need
insulin."

Dean was shocked. What had they done? His
grandma was a diabetic, and from her he knew
that a diabetic could fall into a coma, if they didn't
get their insulin or anything to eat and drink for a
longer span of time. Phil needed sugar. He opened
a bottle of lemonade and held it to Phil's lips.

"Drink", he whispered. "That'll do you good."

Phil couldn't raise her head, so Dean carefully helped her. He had put the torch on the floor so
70 that Phil couldn't see his face. Phil drank a little and then lay down on the cold floor again and closed her eyes.

He offered Phil a sandwich, but she turned her head away.

75 Dean was frightened. He didn't want to be responsible if Phil fell into a coma. He had to think. And then he had to do something.

14. Blame

Cindy
Matt
Dean

"You did what?" Cindy shouted. She could not believe what Dean had just told her. "You saw big fat Philly? You idiot! Why couldn't you leave her alone to rot in that storeroom?"

5 "Don't shout at me", Dean shouted back. "Thanks to Matt Mr Ashton has already died. It was on the news this morning."

"So he can't talk anymore, can he?" Matt said. "Nobody knows that we lit the fire now. And you 10 don't want to threaten that, Dean, do you?"

"Phil is a diabetic", Dean answered. "She could fall into a coma, and I don't want to be responsible for another death."

"I don't care", Matt replied.

15 They were sitting in Dean's room. Dean had asked them to come to his house because he wanted to talk to them about Phil.

"How can you be so heartless, Matt?" Dean asked. "After all you killed Mr Ashton. He has got a family, 20 you know."

"I don't care", Matt repeated. "The most important thing for me is that he can't tell the police about us. It's a shame that the school didn't burn down completely."

"There was a lot of damage", Dean said. "I was there and saw it. At least three classrooms were destroyed. That's what we wanted, isn't it?

"No, that's not what we wanted", Matt answered. "Three classrooms are not enough. We could go and set fire to the place once more. Finish the job, you know. And burn that stupid cow in the storeroom."

"Yes, you're right", Cindy agreed.

Dean was shocked when he heard that Matt and Cindy had no scruples to kill another person and to cause even more damage. He had always thought that Matt and Cindy were his friends, but now he knew they weren't. He didn't want to be the friend of killers.

"You can't do that", he said to them.

"Oh yes, we can", Matt said. "And you will come with us!"

"No, I won't", Dean shouted. "I don't want to have anything more to do with fires and killing people – and I don't want to have anything to do with you anymore."

"Oh really?" Cindy asked.

"Interesting", Matt said. "What do you want to do? Go to the police? You're involved, too. Listen, Dean. If you don't come with us to finish the job and get rid of that cow I'll think of something to make your life really miserable. You've got a motorcycle, right? Something could happen. An accident, perhaps?" Dean couldn't believe his ears.

"That's blackmail", he said.

"Yes, but I don't care", Matt replied. "We'll meet in the park at 11:00 pm tonight. Nobody will expect another fire at Park High School. I'll bring everything we need."

Matt and Cindy left Dean's house.

Dean didn't know what to do. If he informed the police they would sooner or later find out that he, Dean, was one of the arsonists. Perhaps they would blame him for murder, too.

Dean lay down on his bed. Suddenly he was very frightened and started to shiver.

15. Break-in

At 11:00 pm Cindy was already sitting on a bench in the schoolyard when Matt arrived with a big can of petrol in his rucksack. They waited for fifteen minutes, but Dean did not come.

5 "Where's that loser?" Matt asked. "I bet he wet his pants, and he won't come."

Cindy was worried. "Do you think he'll warn the police?" she asked.

"No, I don't think so", Matt answered. "Dean is a
10 sissy."

"And if he makes an anonymous phone call?" Cindy asked.

"If he does that, I'll tell the police that he was involved, too. And, of course, somehow or other
15 I'll make sure he'll never forget me. But I think he's too scared to contact the police."

"I hope you're right", Cindy said. "Okay, where best to set fire to the school – *and* to fat Philly?"

"Well, I thought about that", Matt said. "The boiler
20 room is next to the storeroom in the basement. I think I can open the door with a jimmy, open some valves so that gas can escape, spill the petrol, drop a match – and boom."

"You *do* know that *we* have to get out first, don't
25 you?" Cindy asked. "Can we make it fast enough?"

"Sure. Don't worry, Cindy", Matt tried to calm her. "We start the fire from the hall. By the time the gas ignites, we'll be out of the place."

It was a moonless night, so nobody noticed when
30 Matt and Cindy walked around the school building to find a window to break into. There were no houses at the backside, only a big playground now covered with little puddles of rainwater from the day before. At its end there was a high fence,
35 and behind it the park after which Park High School was named.

Matt smashed a window at the end of a corridor with a hammer until the hole was big enough for them to climb inside.

40 They knew the school well, so they quickly found the stairs down to the basement.

"Ah, here it is", Matt said. "The boiler room."

Matt had no difficulties opening the door to the room with the heating system. He switched on the

45 light.

While Matt started to open a valve with a wrench Cindy asked: "Are we going to have a look at fat Philly?"

"Why?" Matt wanted to know. "No need to do

50 that. She'll hear the bang, and that's it."

"You can't do that", another voice now said behind them. Cindy quickly turned around, and there was Dean.

"We thought you wouldn't make it", Cindy said.

55 "Help Matt with the valves."

"Are you crazy?" Dean cried. "You will blow up the whole building! And you will kill Phil."

"Exactly, sissy", Matt said.

Dean lunged for Matt and wanted to take away his

60 wrench.

"You bloody idiot!" he cried. "Give me that wrench. You are going to kill us all."

fight

Before he knew what was happening Cindy had snatched the wrench out of Matt's hand and hit it

65 on Dean's head. He fell on the floor unconscious.

"Right", she said. "Let's drag him next door to Phil. Now they can die together."

Matt had managed to fully open the valve, and gas was escaping. He put the wrench in his back

70 pocket and helped Cindy to drag Dean along the corridor to the storeroom door.

Cindy switched on the light from the outside and started to unlock the door. She was surprised when she found the door unlocked. She opened it

75 and went inside.

"Matt", she shouted. "Look at this!"

Then he saw it, too. Phil was gone. There was only an empty bottle of lemonade standing in the middle of the room.

80 "Where is she?" Matt asked. "I thought she was half-unconscious and couldn't move."

"I don't know", Cindy answered. "But the door was not locked."

"Do you think that idiot had left it open?" Matt said

85 and pointed at Dean.

"No idea", Cindy replied. "But I'm sure she is here somewhere."

"Probably." Matt said. "Let's put Dean inside the storeroom first, lock the door, finish the job, and

90 get out of here. If Phil is here somewhere she won't
survive.

They locked Dean in the storeroom. Then Matt
took out his canister with the petrol. He opened it
and began to spill the petrol along the corridor
95 while they slowly moved to the stairs, then upstairs
to the hall. Matt opened the entrance door with
the emergency lever and spilled the last of the
petrol. He took out his cigarette lighter and set the
petrol on fire.

16. Fire

Phil smelled the gas that was escaping from the
boiler room. She knew what that meant. Even
switching on a light or a mobile could be dangerous
now and cause an explosion. <u>She knew she had</u>
5 <u>to get out of the building as quickly as possible.</u>
But <u>she had to save Dean first</u>.
Phil was still very weak. She knew that Dean had
brought her the lemonade and given her a drink.
After he had gone she felt better. She found the
10 torch Dean had left. Then she had another drink
from the bottle of lemonade, which helped her to
stabilize her insulin level. Then she fell asleep
again. When she finally woke up she managed to
get up from the floor and moved towards the door.
15 She decided to bang at the door and shout for
help once more. Perhaps someone would hear her
now. But there was no need to bang at the door
and shout for help. When she found the door
handle she instinctively pressed it down – and the
20 door opened. So Dean had not locked it.
She didn't know what time it was but she guessed
it was night because outside in the corridor
everything was dark. She could, however, make
out a locker opposite the storeroom.

25 She was about to find her way along the corridor
to a staircase and out of the building when she
suddenly heard voices.

This time she did not shout. She didn't know if
they belonged to people who came to her rescue
30 or to Dean and his two friends.

She went back to the storeroom door, shut it from
the outside and hid behind the old locker.

Then she heard every word that was spoken. She
recognized the girl now. It was her classmate
35 Cindy. And she recognized Matt, the troublemaker
of her class.

She heard Dean and learned that he wanted to
save her and prevent a catastrophe.

Finally she saw Cindy and Matt dragging Dean
40 into the storeroom and spilling petrol along the
corridor.

She had to act quickly. Now adrenalin worked
through her system. She got up from her hiding
place, ran to the boiler room and shut the door.
45 Then she took off the top of her sweat suit and
jammed it against the bottom end of the door of
the boiler room so that the gas could not get out
into the corridor through the bottom door gap.

She ran to the storeroom and opened it, but she
50 did not switch on the light. She found Dean and
shook him.

Phil

"Dean, wake up! We must get out of here", she cried.

Dean moved, but he didn't say anything.

55 "Dean", Phil cried desperately. "Move! There's going to be a gas explosion! You must help me! Please!"

Dean came around. Slowly he sat up.

"What's happening?" he asked. "Ouch, my head.
60 It hurts so much."

"We must get out of here, Dean! Get up!" Phil commanded.

Suddenly Dean remembered what had happened. He got up, and Phil helped him out into the corridor.
65 Flames were running towards them along the petrol line. It took Dean some time to realize what was going to happen. Then he saw the fire extinguisher near the staircase.

"Get that fire extinguisher", he shouted to Phil. "I
70 can't move so fast."

Phil ran to fetch the extinguisher. Dean took off his leather jacket and tried to beat the flames. He burnt his left hand and dropped the jacket. It caught fire. The flames were only about three or
75 four metres from the boiler room door.

Phil came back with the fire extinguisher. She gave it to Dean and he sprayed the foam on the flames. They couldn't stop the whole fire but the flames stopped running towards the boiler room.

80 "Quick Phil", Dean cried. "Let's run outside. There is still danger of explosion."

Phil and Dean moved along the burning petrol line upstairs to the entrance hall of Park High School as quickly as they could. Phil coughed a lot 85 because of the smoke, and her legs felt weak. She was afraid that she would fall. Dean's head wound was bleeding and hurt so much that he felt dizzy. Finally they reached the main entrance. As soon as they breathed the cold night air they both sat 90 down on the cool schoolyard and embraced.

"Thanks for saving my life", Dean said.

"Thanks for saving mine", Phil answered.

An explosion followed. Windows broke and shards of glass rained on Phil and Dean.

95 The whole school building was on fire.

17. Safe

Dean and Phil spent the night in hospital. They both had mild concussions and lots of small cuts on their heads, backs, arms and legs from the shards of glass from the school windows.

5 Mr and Mrs Doherty sat at Phil's bedside until she fell asleep early on Sunday morning. They also visited Dean in his room to thank him for saving their daughter from falling into a coma, even though he had helped to lock her in the storeroom.

10 Detective Inspector Garner interviewed Dean the next morning. Two police cars were sent to Matt's and to Cindy's houses. Both were arrested for arson and homicide and taken to a juvenile prison. It took the fire brigade hours to get the fire at Park 15 High School under control.

"We'll have to go to another school, big sister", Natalie said when the family picked up Phil from hospital the next morning. "I wonder where."

"I don't care", Phil said. "As long as I'm fine and 20 alive I'll go anywhere."

Then Dean and his father came into the room. Dean's head and hand were bandaged, but he looked happy.

"Phil", he began. "I'd like to tell you how sorry I am 25 for what happened to you in the first place. I was very stupid and I wanted to show Cindy and Matt how tough I was. But it was all wrong."

"Don't worry, Dean", Phil said. "I'm glad we're here and safe. I only feel very sorry for Mr Ashton
30 and his family."

"Me too", Dean said. "My dad and I will see his family as soon as possible."

Then Phil asked: "What will happen to you now?"

"Well", Dean answered. "There's going to be a trial
35 in which I have to testify. I was part of the gang, but I didn't hurt or kill anybody, and I didn't set any of the fires. But, of course, I'll be punished, too."

"Yes", Dean's father said, "but he won't have to go to prison."

40 "And I can't come back to Park High School when it reopens again", Dean added. "I'm expelled."

"I am going to testify, too", Phil said. "And I'll tell them that you rescued me and that you didn't want to blow up the school. I heard all that you
45 and the others said when I was hiding behind the locker."

"Thank you, Phil", Dean said. "You're a great girl. I'm sorry I haven't noticed earlier. Perhaps one day we can meet and have a drink."

50 "Yes", Phil replied. "Perhaps".

Vocabulary

5'6" = 5 foot 6 inches	*ca. 1,68 Meter (Maßeinheit: 1 Fuß = 30,48 cm)*
(to) agree	*zustimmen*
annoying	*nervig, lästig*
argument	*Streit, Meinungsverschiedenheit*
arsonist	*Brandstifter*
at the ready	*bereit*
barbecue	*Grillparty*
basement	*Keller*
(to) be dead worried (was, been)	*ernsthaft besorgt sein*
(to) be due (was, been)	*fällig sein*
(to) be involved (was, been)	*beteiligt sein*
(to) be nuts (was, been)	*eine Macke haben, spinnen*
(to) be on guard (was, been)	*auf Wache sein*
(to) be overweight (was, been)	*übergewichtig sein*
(to) be upset (was, been)	*aufgeregt sein*
bin	*Abfalleimer*

blackmail	Erpressung
(to) blame sb.	jemanden beschuldigen
blockhead	Dummkopf, Schwachkopf
blow	Schlag
boiler room	Heizungsraum
bruised	geprellt
(to) burst into flames (burst, burst)	in Flammen aufgehen
charcoaled	verkohlt
clue	Spur
(to) come around (came, come)	zu sich kommen
concussion	Gehirnerschütterung
(to) consider sth.	etwas erwägen, in Betracht ziehen
(to) console sb.	jemanden trösten
(to) cough	husten
coughing fit	Hustenanfall
(to) crawl	kriechen
cricket bat	Cricketschläger
crime scene tape	Absperrband
(to) croak	krächzen
(to) demand	fordern
deserted	verlassen
(to) deserve sth.	etwas verdienen

desperate	*verzweifelt*
diabetes	*Diabetes (= Stoffwechsel-erkrankung)*
disappearance	*Verschwinden*
(to) discover	*entdecken*
(to) distribute	*verteilen*
dizzy	*schwindelig, benommen*
(to) do sb. a favour (did, done)	*jemandem einen Gefallen tun*
(to) drag (dragged, dragged)	*ziehen, schleppen*
embarrassed	*beschämt*
(to) embrace	*sich umarmen*
emergency lever	*Nothebel*
(to) escape	*hier: ausströmen*
(to) expel (expelled, expelled)	*verweisen, hinauswerfen*
(to) explore	*erkunden*
(to) fancy so. (fancied, fancied)	*jemanden gern mögen; auf jemanden stehen*
fiercely	*heftig*
(to) file a missing person's report	*eine Vermisstenanzeige aufgeben*
fire extinguisher	*Feuerlöscher*
foam	*Schaum*
furthest from	*am weitesten entfernt von*

GCSE	*General Certificate of Secondary Education = ein Schulabschluss, der mit der mittleren Reife vergleichbar ist*
(to) get rid of sb. or sth. (got, got)	*jemanden oder etwas los werden*
glimpse	*kurzer, flüchtiger Blick*
guilt	*Schuld*
gusts of wind	*Windböen, Windstöße*
handrail	*Geländer*
hardly	*kaum*
heating system	*Heizungsanlage*
(to) hesitate	*zögern*
homicide	*Totschlag*
hood	*Kapuze*
(to) ignite	*sich entzünden*
in the first place	*zuerst, ursprünglich*
(to) inject	*injizieren, spritzen*
insulin	*Insulin (= Hormon, das den Blutzuckerspiegel senkt)*
(to) investigate	*untersuchen, ermitteln*
(to) jam (jammed, jammed)	*einklemmen, verstopfen*
jimmy	*Brecheisen*
(to) join sb.	*sich jemandem anschließen*

juvenile prison	*Jugendvollzugsanstalt*
(to) lift	*(an)heben*
lighter	*Feuerzeug*
lightning	*Blitz*
(to) lunge for sb.	*sich auf jemanden stürzen*
mackintosh	*Regenmantel*
(to) misbehave	*sich schlecht benehmen*
neighbourhood	*hier: Wohnviertel*
nickname	*Spitzname*
petrol-soaked	*benzingetränkt*
(to) plead	*bitten, flehen*
(to) pour	*schütten, gießen*
(to) prefer (preferred, preferred)	*bevorzugen*
(to) prevent	*verhindern*
purse	*Geldbörse*
ransom	*Lösegeld*
(to) realize	*erkennen, feststellen*
(to) recharge	*wieder aufladen (eine Batterie/einen Akku)*
(to) recognize	*wiedererkennen*
relationship	*Beziehung*
rescue	*Rettung*
responsible	*verantwortlich*
rolling thunder	*grollender Donner*

scruple	*Skrupel, Bedenken*
severe	*ernst, schlimm*
shard	*Scherbe, Glassplitter*
shelter	*Schutz, Unterstand*
(to) shiver	*zittern, schaudern, frösteln*
(to) shriek	*aufschreien*
sissy	*Weichei*
smoke poisoning	*Rauchvergiftung*
(to) snatch sth.	*etwas packen, entreißen*
(to) sob (sobbed, sobbed)	*schluchzen*
somehow or other	*irgendwie*
(to) stare	*starren*
stone	*hier: Gewichtseinheit: 1 stone entspricht 6,35 kg*
storeroom	*Lagerraum*
(to) stumble	*stolpern*
successful	*erfolgreich*
(to) suspect	*verdächtigen*
sweat suit	*Trainingsanzug*
(to) testify (testified, testified)	*aussagen, bezeugen*
(to) threaten	*(be)drohen*
tool case	*Werkzeugkasten*
top of the stairs	*oberes Treppenende*

torch	*Taschenlampe*
tough	*hart im Nehmen sein, knallhart*
trial	*Prozess, Gerichtsverhandlung*
unconscious	*bewusstlos*
valve	*Ventil*
(to) wail	*heulen*
wanna	*umgangssprachlich für: do you want to*
weak	*schwach*
(to) well up	*aufwallen, hervorquellen*
What the heck …	*Was zum Teufel …*
whoomph	*ein plötzliches lautes Geräusch wie von einer Explosion*
wing	*Flügel*
(to) work off	*abreagieren, Stress abbauen*
wrench	*Schraubenschlüssel*
yard	*Längenmaß: 1 yard entspricht 0,914 m*
yet	*hier: dennoch*

Bildquellen

Seite 5:   junge, leicht übergewichtige Frau,
             © Hugo Félix – Fotolia.com

Seite 8:   langer Flur in einem Schulgebäude,
             © nothing1223 – Fotolia.com

Seite 13:   ohnmächtiger Mann, © pixelaway –
             Fotolia.com

Seite 14:   Frau sieht aus dem Fenster, © dubova –
             Fotolia.com

Seite 18:   gesichtslose Person, © igor –
             Fotolia.com

Seite 24:   Feuerwehrmann im Einsatz,
             © karelnoppe – Fotolia.com

Seite 26:   Paar, das sich an den Händen hält,
             © LoloStock – Fotolia.com

Seite 29:   Silhouette eines weiblichen Teenagers,
             © Chris Tefme – Fotolia.com

Seite 32:   zwei Teenager, die sich streiten,
             © karelnoppe – Fotolia.com

Seite 36:   Treppenhaus, © Bruno Bernier –
             Fotolia.com

Seite 43:   Smartphone mit Hülle, © tetxu –
             Fotolia.com

Seite 48:	ohnmächtige junge Frau, © Photo_Ma – Fotolia.com
Seite 54:	Einbrecher, der ein Fenster einschlägt, © Chlorophylle – Fotolia.com
Seite 61:	Flammen, © flukesamed – Fotolia.com